A New True Book

THE CHOCTAW

By Emilie U. Lepthien

Consultant: Robert B. Ferguson
Tribal Historian
Mississippi Band of Choctaw

CHILDRENS PRESS ®

CHICAGO

PHOTO CREDITS

© Julie Kelsey—2, 29 (2 photos), 32 (right), 45 (bottom right)

© Emilie Lepthien—2, 7 (2 photos), 17, 19 (right), 24, 28 (2 photos), 30, 31 (2 photos), 32 (left), 33 (2 photos), 34 (2 photos), 35 (2 photos), 45 (upper right)

Mississippi State Historical Museum—19 (left)

Mississippi Department of Archives and History—12

The Newberry Library, Chicago—21

New Orleans Museum of Art—4

The Oklahoma Historical Society—11

Photri—14

© John Running Photographs—8, 9, 23, (2 photos), 26, 36 (2 photos), 37 (2 photos), 38 (2 photos), 41, 42 (2 photos), 43 (3 photos), 45 (left)

To the Choctaw Indians, who have faced every adversity but retained their culture, pride, and honor.

Library of Congress Cataloging-in-Publication Data

Lepthien, Emilie U. (Emilie Uttig)
The Choctaw.

(A New true book)
Includes index.
Summary: A brief history of the Choctaw Indian tribe.
1. Choctaw Indians—Juvenile literature.
[1. Choctaw Indians. 2. Indians of North America]
I. Title.
E99.C8L47 1987 973'.0497 87-14583
ISBN 0-516-01240-1

FIFTH PRINTING 1992
Childrens Press®, Chicago

Printed in the United States of America.
5 6 7 8 9 10 R 96 95 94 93 92

TABLE OF CONTENTS

This painting, done by Alfred Boisseau in 1847, shows ancestors of the Choctaw walking along a bayou (marshy inlet of a river or lake).

THE PEACEFUL CHOCTAW

Chahta Hapia Hoke, "We are the Choctaw," a proud nation declares.

For generations the Choctaw lived in Alabama and Mississippi. The legends of the Choctaw told their tribal history. One legend told about how the Choctaw chose a place to settle.

The tribe came from the northwest. The prophets

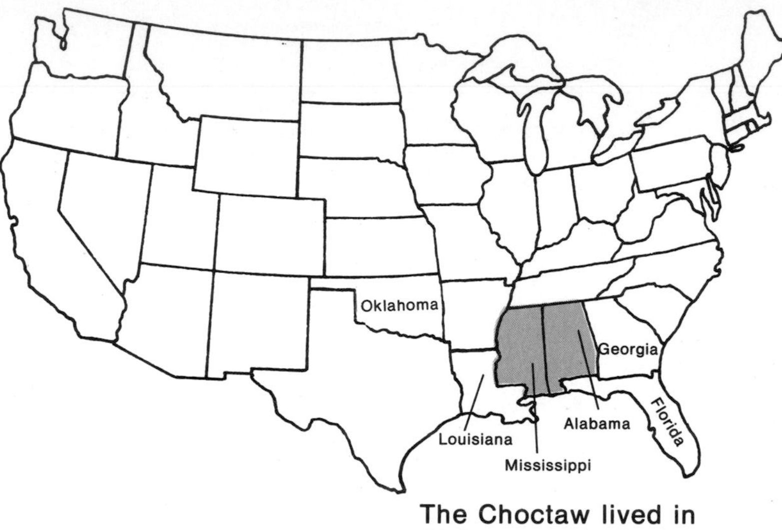

The Choctaw lived in Alabama and Mississippi.

had said there was fertile land and good hunting in the east. Their leader, Chahta, carried a sacred pole. The sacred pole would tell them where to settle.

Each night Chahta drove the pole into the ground. Each morning the pole

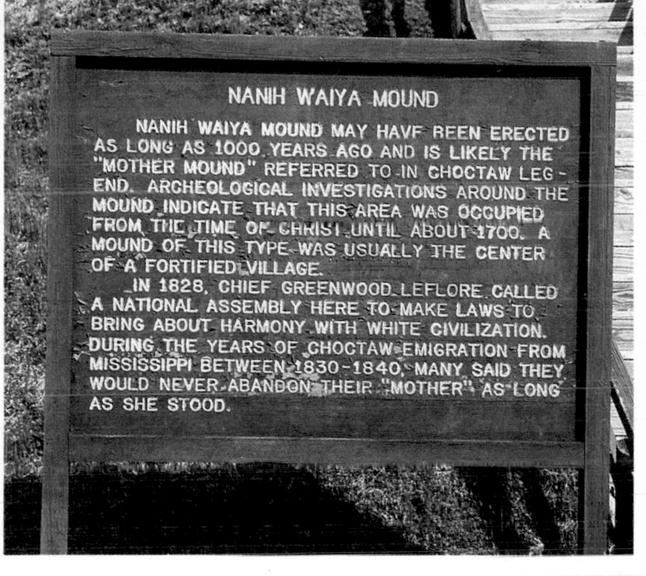

Nanih Waiya Mound, as it is today

leaned to the east. Finally, at Nanih Waiya the pole stood upright. Chahta said this was the place to stay. There they built their homes and a sacred burial mound. Some Choctaw live near Nanih Waiya, Mississippi, today.

PEACEFUL TIMES

Hickory nuts, walnuts, and pecans

The Choctaw lived peacefully as farmers for hundreds of years. They raised corn, beans, squash, and pumpkins. Farm tools were made from stone, wood, or bone.

They gathered fruits, nuts, and berries. They hunted wild game with bows and arrows. The

A blowgun, made from swamp cane, was used to hunt small game.

boys used blowguns to bring down birds. Fish were caught with nets, spears, and arrows.

The Choctaw never wasted food. They shared extra corn, fish, and game with neighbors. The forest was precious. They made only narrow paths through the trees.

To build their cabins they drove poles close together into the ground. The poles were tied together with strong vines. Strips of cane filled the spaces between poles. Then mud was used to cover the cane. Roofs were thatched or covered with cypress or pine bark. Holes in the roof let the smoke out.

Clay bowl from the 1830s

Cooking was done mostly outdoors in earthen pots over an open fire. Dishes and spoons were made of wood, shells, or bison horns.

Beds lined the walls. They were raised and covered with cane. The beds also served as tables and chairs.

A Choctaw sharecropper family in 1937

These hardworking farmers were peaceful. But they fought fiercely when they were attacked.

INTRUDERS ON THEIR LAND

In 1540 strange men entered Choctaw land. Some of the men rode animals. The Choctaw had never seen horses. They had never seen armor.

The strange men were from Spain. Their leader was Hernando De Soto.

At Maubilia, the Spaniards fought the

Hernando De Soto in Mississippi, 1541

Mobile Choctaw. The Indians fought bravely. But their arrows could not cut through Spanish armor. Hundreds of Choctaw men were killed, but the battle stopped the Spaniards' attack.

For another 150 years

the Choctaw had few contacts with white men. But by 1700, there were white settlers nearby.

For a time, the Choctaw were under the control of French governors. Then in 1763, the land came under British rule.

European settlers later called the Choctaw one of the Five Civilized Tribes. The Five Civilized Tribes were the Choctaw, Creek, Cherokee, Seminole, and Chickasaw.

AN INDEPENDENT NATION

In January 1786, the United States government recognized the independent Choctaw Nation.

Four acts of Congress regulated relations between the Choctaws and settlers. Hunting and

River near Nanih Waiya

settling on Indian lands was forbidden. The Choctaws thought they had found a government that would guarantee their rights.

EDUCATION AND RELIGION

The Choctaw asked for a Christian mission by 1819. Missionaries Cyrus Byington and Alfred Wright worked with the Folsoms, two Choctaw men.

Together they translated part of the Bible and hymns into Choctaw. Reverend Byington also put together a Choctaw

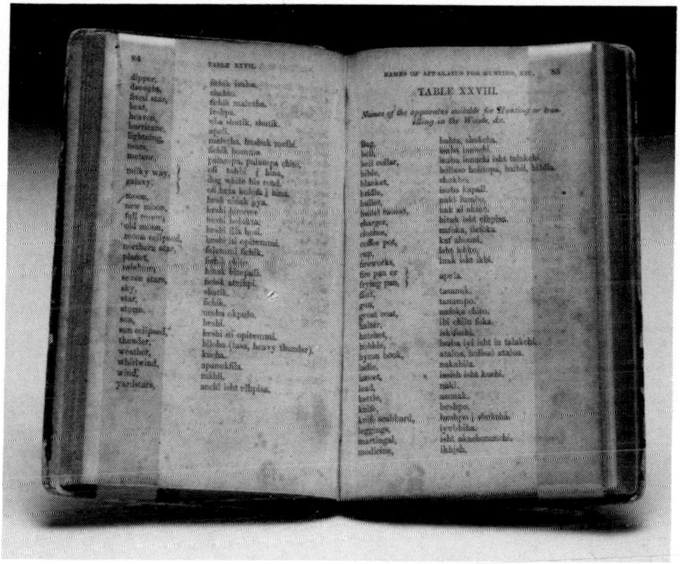

First Choctaw dictionary, 1852 (left). Today, Choctaw children learn from books printed in their native language (right) as well as in English.

grammar, speller, and dictionary.

The missionaries started schools. By 1830 there were 11 schools, 29 teachers, and 260 students. About 250 adults were being taught to read their native language.

MORE TREATIES

The Choctaw Nation had adopted laws based on United States law.

From 1801 to 1830, six more treaties were signed. Each time, the Choctaw gave up more land to the United States. President Andrew Jackson wanted the land for American settlers. In the 1820 treaty, more land in the West was opened to settlers.

Pushmataha, a Choctaw chief, took part in treaty negotiations between the Choctaw Nation and the United States.

In the 1830 Treaty of Dancing Rabbit Creek, the Choctaw Nation lost the last of its eastern land. They were told to move to Indian Territory (Oklahoma). In all, they traded 23 million acres in Mississippi for 13 million acres in Oklahoma.

About 20,000 Choctaw lost land by this treaty. Over 8,000 decided to stay in Mississippi and claim land.

On the 350-mile journey to Indian Territory, one-fourth of the 12,000 Choctaw died of hunger, disease, and bitter winter weather. When they reached their new land, they had no tools, cattle, or seed to begin farming.

INDIAN TERRITORY

Finally, when they could farm, the hardworking Choctaw raised pecans, cotton, corn, and other vegetables. They traded some crops for other goods.

Hickory corn (below) and a primitive corn used in making popcorn (left) are displayed in baskets made from swamp cane.

Head Start classroom at Pearl River Reservation

They started schools. The Choctaw wanted to learn English.

Fortunately, however, they continued to speak, read, and write in Choctaw in both Oklahoma and Mississippi.

PROBLEMS ARISE

When the Civil War began, the Choctaw sided with the Southern states. However, they did little fighting.

When the South was defeated, the Choctaw resumed relations with the United States. But things had changed. Many of the Choctaw families were very poor. While the men had been in the army, thieves had taken their cattle.

Choctaw clothing of 1911

Their villages in Oklahoma were attacked by Plains Indians.

By 1907, the Choctaw Nation in the west became a part of the state of Oklahoma. It was no longer independent.

THE EASTERN OR MISSISSIPPI BAND OF CHOCTAW

The Mississippi Band lived in poverty. By 1900 many were sharecroppers. The land they had once owned (nearly 500 square miles) had been taken away.

By 1930 only 1,162 Choctaw lived in Mississippi. Today there

The office of the tribal chief at Pearl River Reservation (left) is separate from other tribal offices (right).

are about 6,000. The Eastern Choctaw live in seven small reservation communities near Philadelphia, Mississippi. The land is held in trust by the U.S. government. A land of hills and ravines, it is not good for modern farming methods.

Choctaw Central High School Homecoming Queen (left)
and Tribal Chief Phillip Martin (right)

Phillip Martin was elected chief of the Mississippi Band. He saw the need to preserve tribal culture by making the reservation self-sufficient.

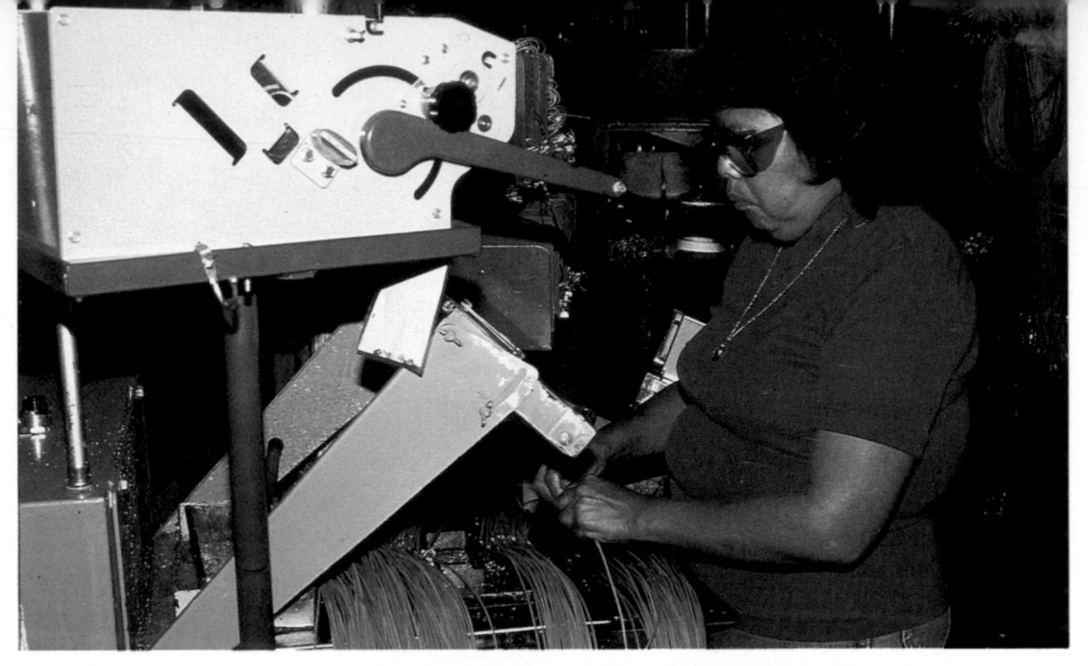

A worker prepares wires to be installed in automobile electrical systems.

He contacted large companies. He told them that the Choctaw were hard workers. Today there are factories where such different items as electrical wiring for cars and trucks, radio speakers, and greeting cards are

This greeting card factory is one of several small industries located in an Industrial Park area of the reservation.

assembled. Hundreds of Choctaw are employed.

The Mississippi Band has buses to bring the Choctaw from their communities to the factories at Pearl River, Redwater, and DeKalb.

The tribe also has buildings for job training,

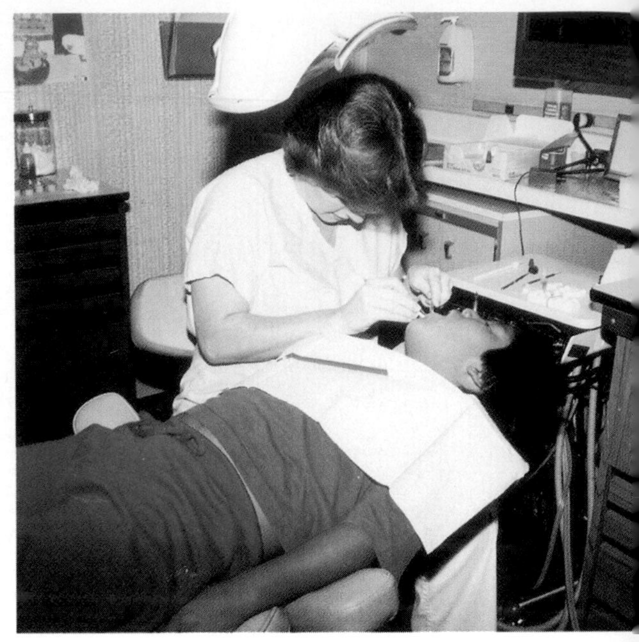

New housing, built by tribal workers (left), and a dental clinic (right)

food distribution, and bus maintenance. The tribe's development company has built six hundred new homes and renovated over 100 more. Classrooms, community buildings, and the Choctaw Health Center were built by this tribal

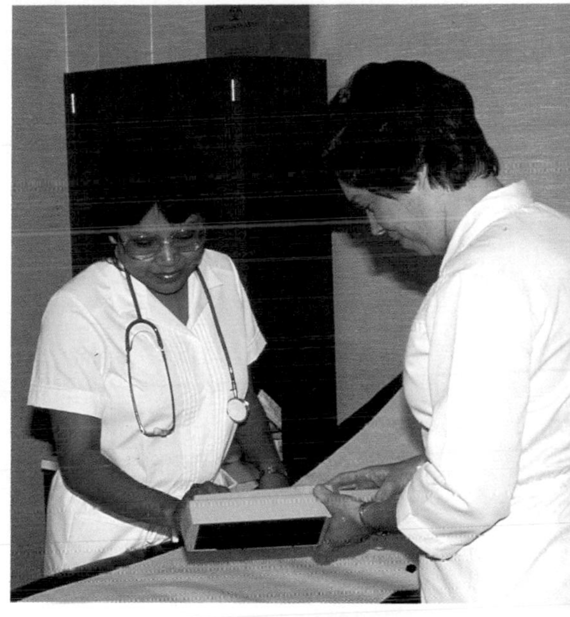

The Choctaw health center (left) and a nurse's aid (above)

company. There are plans to build a shopping center too.

A modern hospital and health care center is operated by the tribe. A new home for retired senior citizens is planned.

Each year during Arbor Week, the tribe plants oak and pine seedlings.

Pine trees are cut down and made into paper pulp. The tribe plants as many as 40,000 Florida slash pine seedlings in a year. Twenty years from now they will be ready to cut.

Day care, Head Start, elementary schools, a high

The Bureau of Indian Affairs operates the public school on Pearl River Reservation (left). An elementary school on the Bogue Chitto Reservation (right)

school, and adult education classes serve the people. There are several churches.

Each year since 1949, the Mississippi Band holds a Choctaw Indian Fair. In this way they preserve their heritage and culture. The young men play

Among the many activities taking place at the annual Choctaw Indian Fair are stickball (left) and basket weaving (right).

stickball, the oldest ball game in America. Many people exhibit their beadwork and basketry. Tribal dances and songs are performed. The women wear their traditional multicolored dresses,

Colorfully dressed dancers (left) respond to the chants of traditional singers (right).

ribbons, and beads. The men wear colorful shirts, black felt hats, and belts trimmed with ribbons.

In World War I, Choctaw soldiers spoke Choctaw when they radioed information to the soldiers

The tribe honors its soldiers (right), who have fought bravely in war, as well as its elders (above), who preserve the wisdom and history of the tribe.

in the front lines. The Germans heard these radio messages, but could not understand the Choctaw "code." The Choctaw soldiers helped America win battles.

CHOCTAW NATION OF OKLAHOMA

The Choctaw population in Oklahoma is now about 20,000. Their first capitol was built in 1838 at Tuskahoma. Rebuilt twice, it is now a museum. The present headquarters is at Durant. The chief is Hollis E. Roberts. There are seven field officers in other counties.

The tribe owns and operates Arrowhead Resort Hotel on a lovely lake. Since 1978, there have been Head Start programs. The hospital in Talihina is run by the Choctaw Nation.

The Board of Agriculture operates a 2,627-acre ranch. Nutrition, food distribution, senior citizen services, social services, housing, and education are important Choctaw programs.

CULTURE

Every Labor Day weekend, the tribe holds a festival at Tuskahoma.

Festival dances honor the eagle, duck, quail, raccoon, and snake. Both men and women dance.

Teams from different areas compete in the annual stickball tournament. Each team has its own drummer (far right) to provide support.

A chanter leads the dancers. The only instruments are the drum and sticks for beating together.

Stickball games are played. The ball is made of deerskin or cowhide. Hickory sticks, or *kapucha*,

Stickball is played with two small sticks (top left) and a ball made from strips of cowhide or deerskin (above).

three feet long, are used. A team scores when it scoops up the ball and throws or touches it against its own goalpost.

Stickball world championships are held each year in Mississippi.

GOVERNMENT

Both the Mississippi and Oklahoma Choctaw elect a chief and members of a tribal council. In 1945 the Mississippi Band approved its constitution. The Choctaw Nation of Oklahoma ratified its constitution in 1983.

Both groups administer most of their own affairs. There are small groups of Choctaw in Louisiana, Tennessee, and Illinois.

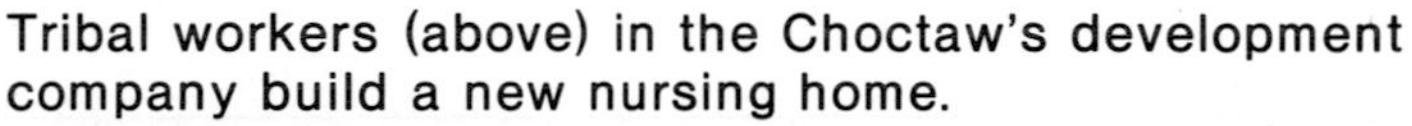

Tribal workers (above) in the Choctaw's development company build a new nursing home.

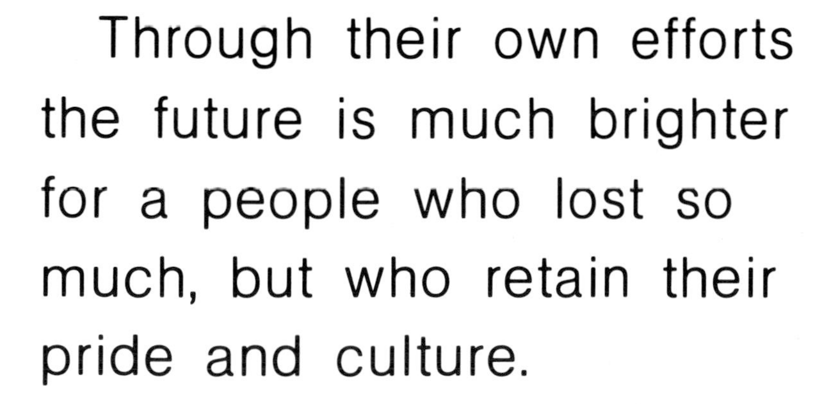

Through their own efforts the future is much brighter for a people who lost so much, but who retain their pride and culture.

SOME CHOCTAW WORDS

Choctaw is a Muskogan language related to Creek, Chickasaw, Seminole, and Miccosukee.

Oklahoma (okla homa)
Red people

Tuscaloosa (tushka lusa)
Black Warrior

Neshoba (Nushoba)
Wolf

Bogalusa (Bok lusa)
Black River

Bogue Chitto (Bok Chitto)
Big River

Talahina (tali hina—rock road) Railroad

FAMOUS CHOCTAW CHIEFS

Tuscaloosa:
Tricked Hernando De Soto

Mushulatubbee:
Encouraged children to attend school in 1819

Pushmataha:
Died in Washington, D.C., in 1824 while negotiating a treaty regarding Choctaw land.

WORDS YOU SHOULD KNOW

adopted(uh • DOP • tid) — accepted, taken over, made as one's own

chanter(CHAN • ter) — a singer; one who sings a simple song that has many words or syllables sung on each note

code(KOHD) — system of letters or words or signals that has a secret meaning

defeated(dih • FEE • tid) — beaten; overcome

generation(jen • uh • RAY • shun) — the average period of time between births of parents and children or children and grandchildren, usually considered to be about 30 years

independent(in • dih • PEN • dint) — free, able to manage by oneself

journey(JER • nee) — a trip, travel

mound(MOUND) — a small hill, natural or created, of earth, sand, or gravel; burial ground

native(NAY • tiv) — born or living naturally in a certain place

poverty(PAHV • er • tee) — state of being poor

ravine(ruh • VEEN) — a deep, narrow valley, usually cut into the earth by flowing water

renovated(REN • oh • vay • tid) — repaired, made as new again

reservation(rez • er • VAY • shun) — land reserved by the government for special use, as for an Indian tribe

resumed(rih • ZOOMD) — started again; taken up where one stopped

self-sufficient(SELF suh • FISH • uhnt) — able to provide for one's own support and upkeep

sharecropper(SHAR • krop • er) — tenant farmer who shares the crop with the landlord in payment of rent for the farmland

thatched(THATCHD) — covered with straw, reeds, or large leaves, as a thatched roof

trust(TRUHST) — a legal title to property held by one party for the benefit of another

vine(VYN) — a plant having firm but slender, easily twisted stems

INDEX

About the author

Emilie Utteg Lepthien earned BS and MA degrees and a certificate in school administration from Northwestern University. She has worked as an upper-grade science and social studies teacher supervisor and as principal of an elementary and upper-grade center for twenty years. Ms. Lepthien has also written and narrated science and social studies scripts for the Radio Council of the Chicago Board of Education.

Ms. Lepthien was awarded the American Educator's Medal by Freedoms Foundation. She is a member of the Delta Kappa Gamma Society International, Chicago Principals Association, and life member of the NEA. She has been a co-author of primary social studies texts for Rand, McNally and Co., and an educational consultant for Encyclopaedia Britannica Films. Ms. Lepthien has written Enchantment of the World books on Australia, Ecuador, and the Philippines for Childrens Press.